Baking Without flour

RECIPES FOR MICROWAVE AND AIR FRYER

Carlos Medrano

Acknowledgments

Thank you for embarking on this adventurous journey with me through this daring recipe book, which has been a joy to create and bring to you.

Thanks to all those who have shared the recipes on social media because without their help, this wouldn't be possible.

Thanks to my family and friends for motivating me.

Thanks to you for reading... enjoy the recipes.

Prologue

As the Great Gusteau said (a character from Disney's 2007 movie Ratatouille), "Anyone can cook," and indeed, anyone can do it, and it's much easier with a guide. **"BAKING WITHOUT FLOUR"** is not a cookbook intended to be a weight-loss book, but it could serve as a supplement if your nutritionist prohibits the consumption of refined flour.

The recipes you will find here are easy to make, and as the book's title suggests, they exclude refined wheat flour and make use of flours like oat, coconut, almonds, among others.

For the baking in this book, you can use your microwave or air fryer, thus replacing the conventional gas oven. Most of the recipes are for individual portions.

Without further ado, I invite you to randomly choose one of the recipes and enjoy the texture and flavor without guilt.

Karo
maple

Contents

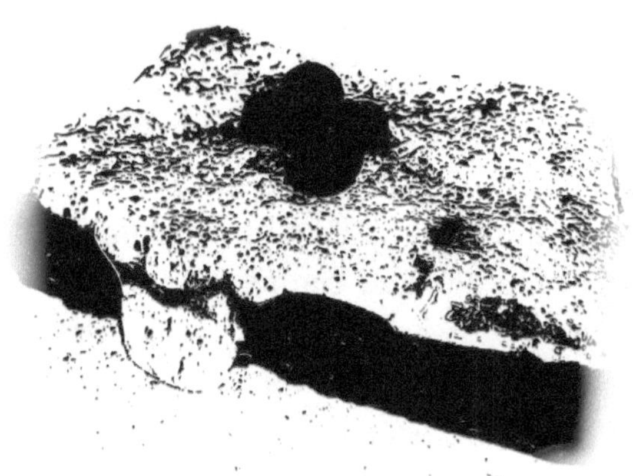

Oatmeal Pancakes

Ingredients:

1 cup of oats
1 banana
½ cup of almond milk
1 egg
1 tablespoon of vanilla

Instructions:

1.-Blend oats, banana, milk, egg, and vanilla to create a batter; it should have a thick consistency.

2.-Heat a skillet and grease it with a little coconut oil.

3.-Take some batter using a ladle and form the pancakes on the skillet. Let them cook for 3 minutes on each side, and serve the oatmeal pancakes.

I hope you enjoy the recipe.

Banana and Oat Bread

Ingredients:

2 eggs
2 bananas
1 teaspoon vanilla extract
1 teaspoon baking powder (Rexal)
2 cups oats
1/2 cup olive oil
1/2 cup brown sugar
A pinch of salt

Instructions:

1. Mash the bananas and set them aside.
2. In a bowl, beat the two eggs, add the vanilla extract, olive oil, salt, baking powder, and finally the mashed bananas. Then, add the two cups of oats and mix.
3. Grease a pan or use parchment paper in a mold and place it in the air fryer for 20 minutes at 350°F (175°C). You can top the mixture with nuts, chia seeds, or granola.

Apple Dessert

Ingredients:

2 eggs
2 small apples
50 grams of Greek yogurt
1 teaspoon of baking powder (Rexal)
*Cinnamon for topping, optional

Instructions:

1. Pour all the ingredients into a blender and blend for two minutes.

2. In a microwave-safe bowl, add the mixture and cook for 8 minutes.

3. If you prefer using a conventional oven, it is recommended to bake at 190°C (375°F) for 30 minutes.

Gluten-Free Peanut Butter Bread

Ingredients:

1 egg
1 tablespoon of peanut butter
1 tablespoon of baking powder (Rexal)
A pinch of salt

Instructions:

1. Pour all the ingredients into a bowl and mix until well combined.

2. Transfer the mixture into a small greased container and place it in a conventional oven or an air fryer.

3. Bake for 10 to 15 minutes at 180°C (350°F) in a conventional oven.

4. In an air fryer, bake for 10 minutes at 180°C (350°F).

Note: Quantities are for an individual-sized bread.

Green Plantain Fit Bread

Ingredients:

1 green plantain (240g)
2 eggs 2 tablespoons of Safflower or olive oil
1 tablespoon of baking powder Salt and oregano
to taste

Preparation:

1. Blend the ingredients and pour the mixture into a 20x10 mold. Bake for 30 minutes at 180° Celsius.

2. In an air fryer, cook for 25 minutes at 180° Celsius.

Oat and Banana Cookies

Ingredients:

1 ripe banana

1 cup of oats

1/2 cup of shredded coconut

2 eggs

1 tablespoon of baking powder (Rexal)
Cinnamon to taste Optional sweetener or honey

Preparation:

1. Mix all the ingredients in a bowl, and once well combined, use a spoon to scoop portions that you place and flatten slightly on a greased baking sheet.

2. You should get approximately 8 cookies. Place pieces of nuts on top.

3. Bake in a conventional oven for 10 minutes at 180 degrees Celsius.

Express Tiramisu

Ingredients:

1 egg
1 cup of oats
1 tablespoon of baking powder (Rexal)
2 tablespoons of Greek yogurt
1 packet of stevia (artificial sweetener)

Preparation:

1. Grease a small container and pour in the mixture. Microwave for 2 minutes or air fry at 180 degrees Celsius (356°F) for 6 to 7 minutes.

2. For the topping, use sweetened Greek yogurt with stevia.

3. Once out of the oven, cut it in half and poke it with a toothpick, then drizzle a little black coffee over it. Place a layer of the yogurt topping and put the lid on to repeat the same procedure. Finally, sprinkle with cocoa.

Microwave Carrot Cake

Ingredients:

1/4 cup of olive oil
1 egg
1/4 cup of oat flour
1 tablespoon of cinnamon
1 tablespoon of baking powder (Rexal)
1 yogurt (medium-sized container)
1/2 cup of grated carrot
1 packet of stevia (artificial sweetener)
A splash of vanilla extract

Preparation:

1. Mix all the ingredients in a bowl and pour them into a greased mold.

2. Microwave for 4 minutes.

Cocoa and Banana Sponge Cake

Ingredients:

1 banana
1 egg
2 small tablespoons of cocoa
3 small tablespoons of shredded coconut
1 tablespoon of baking powder (Rexal)

Preparation:

1. Mix everything in a microwave-safe container and microwave for 3 and a half minutes.

Fit Brownie

Ingredients:

1 banana
1 egg
2 small tablespoons of cocoa
1 teaspoon of baking powder (Rexal)
1 splash of vanilla extract
1 packet of Stevia (artificial sweetener)
*Optional chopped nuts and pieces of dark chocolate.

Preparation:

1. Mash the banana and mix it with the rest of the ingredients, including nuts.

2. Pour the mixture into a container and top it with pieces of chocolate.

3. Microwave for 3 minutes.

Carrot Crepes

Ingredients:

100 grams of carrot
1 egg
200 grams of egg whites
110 grams of oats
A pinch of salt

Preparation:

1. Pour all the ingredients into a blender and blend for three minutes. If the mixture is too thick, add a little water.

2. In a non-stick skillet, pour the mixture to cover the surface of the pan, which should be over medium heat on the stove.

Banana and Yogurt Cake

Ingredients:

2 bananas (200 grams)
1 1/2 cups of Greek yogurt (400 grams)
4 eggs

Preparation:

1. Place all the ingredients in a blender until you achieve a homogeneous mixture.

2. Pour the mixture into a 15-centimeter mold.

3. Cook in an air fryer for 30 minutes at 170°C. In a conventional gas oven, bake for 40 minutes at 180°C, and in the microwave, cook for 10 minutes in 2-minute intervals.

*After cooling, decorate with cinnamon and bananas.

3-Minute Microwave Donuts

Ingredients:

1 ripe banana

1/4 cup of oat flour (25 grams)

A pinch of cinnamon

1 splash of vanilla extract

1 teaspoon of baking powder (Rexal)

For the topping: 5 pieces of dark chocolate
chunks 1 teaspoon of coconut oil

Preparation:

1. Place the ripe banana in the blender jar,
    add the 25 grams of oat flour, and the rest
    of the ingredients.

2. Pour the mixture into the molds and cook
    at maximum power in the microwave for 2
    and a half minutes.

*   Melt the chocolate and coconut oil in the
    microwave to dip the donuts. Allow them
    to rest in the refrigerator for 5 minutes.

Carrot and Oat Muffin

Ingredients:

2 cups of oats

1 teaspoon of baking powder (Rexal)

2 teaspoons of cinnamon

1/4 cup of walnuts

1 grated carrot

2 eggs

1 1/2 cups of almond milk

Preparation:

1. Mix all the ingredients in a bowl.

2. Fill the previously greased molds with the mixture.

3. Bake in an air fryer or conventional oven for 20 minutes at 180°C.

Air Fryer Apple Muffin

Ingredients:

1/2 apple
2 tablespoons of milk
1 teaspoon of vanilla
1 egg
1 tablespoon of unsweetened Greek yogurt
1/4 cup of oat flour
1 teaspoon of cinnamon
1 teaspoon of baking powder (Rexal)
1 packet of stevia (artificial sweetener)

Preparation:

1. Place the apple, milk, and vanilla in a blender. Blend until you have applesauce, then add the rest of the ingredients.

2. Pour the mixture into a baking mold suitable for the oven and place it in the air fryer at 160 degrees for 20 minutes.

P.S: You can add caramelized apple pieces as a topping.

Cinnamon Apple Muffin

Ingredients:

1 apple
1 egg
30 grams of oat flour
1 tablespoon of baking powder (Rexal)
A small amount of low-fat butter or olive oil,
Stevia to taste, and Cinnamon

Preparation:

1. Peel the apple and cut it into small cubes.
    Place it in a bowl and add cinnamon,
    Stevia, along with the butter, and
    microwave for 2 minutes.

2. In another bowl, mix the egg, oat flour,
    baking powder, cinnamon, and Stevia, and
    mix well.

3. Add the apple pieces to the mixture and
    mix thoroughly. Cook in the microwave
    for 2 to 3 minutes.

Frozen Banana Charlotte

Ingredients:

4 bananas
1 1/2 cups of unsweetened Greek yogurt
1 package of Maria cookies
1 packet of stevia (artificial sweetener) Cajeta
(caramelized goat's milk) and walnuts

Preparation:

1. Blend two bananas with the yogurt, stevia, and vanilla.

2. In a baking dish, place a layer of Maria cookies as the base and pour several spoonfuls of the mixture over them. Add banana slices and cajeta. Repeat the layering process until you finish the mixture.

3. Decorate with sliced banana, chopped Maria cookies, and walnuts. Refrigerate for 3 hours.

Chocolate Oatmeal in 5 Minutes

Ingredients:

1/2 cup of rolled oats
1/2 cup of water
1/2 cup of milk or plant-based milk
1 tablespoon of cocoa and cinnamon powder A splash of vanilla extract

Preparation:

1. Mix all the ingredients in a microwave-safe bowl and add chocolate chips.

2. Microwave for 5 minutes and enjoy.

Chewy Air Fryer Brownie

Ingredients:

1/2 cup of oats
1/2 cup of almond flour
1/4 cup of cocoa powder
1 teaspoon of baking powder (Rexal)
1/2 large banana
1 egg
2 tablespoons of calorie-free sweetener
1/4 cup of almond milk
Chopped cashews Semi-sweet chocolate chips

Preparation:

1. Mix all the ingredients in a bowl, and optionally, add the cashews and chocolate chips.

2. Transfer the mixture to a greased glass baking dish and sprinkle more cashews and chocolate chips on top.

3. In the air fryer, cook at 150°C for 10 minutes, then reduce the temperature to 120°C for an additional 5 minutes.

Microwave Chocolate Bread

Ingredients:

2 small apples
1 egg
1 teaspoon of baking powder (Rexal)
1 teaspoon of instant coffee
A splash of vanilla extract

Preparation:

1. Add the chopped apple and a splash of water to a blender to make applesauce.

2. Add the rest of the ingredients to the blender and mix well to incorporate them.

3. Pour the mixture into a microwave-safe mold, and with chocolate chips on top, cook for 3 minutes.

P.S: It's a single serving.

No-Bake Two-Ingredient Apple Cake

Ingredients:

2 diced apples
20 grams of gelatin

Preparation:

1. Microwave the apple pieces for 4 minutes.

2. Blend them with a little hot water to make applesauce.

3. In a bowl, add the applesauce and the 20 grams of gelatin, beating until it thickens.

4. Place the mixture in a mold on wax paper and refrigerate for a few hours or overnight. You can decorate it with cinnamon as a topping.

Lemon Coconut Bites

Ingredients:

1/3 cup of peanut butter
1 1/2 cups of shredded coconut Lemon zest
1 teaspoon of liquid sweetener

Preparation:

1. Mix the peanut butter with lemon zest, coconut, and the liquid sweetener.

2. Shape the mixture into small balls using your hands and coat them with coconut.

Strawberries in Gelatin

Ingredients:

1 cup of strawberries
1 cup of Greek yogurt
1 packet of artificial sweetener (stevia)
1 packet of gelatin

Preparation:

1. Blend the strawberries with the yogurt and add the artificial sweetener.

2. In four tablespoons of water, sprinkle the gelatin for better dissolution. Microwave for 5 to 10 seconds and stir until completely dissolved.

3. Add the hydrated gelatin to the strawberry mixture and blend for a couple of minutes.

4. Pour the mixture into individual molds or containers and refrigerate for two hours.

Frozen Lemon Pie

Ingredients:

30 crushed marvel cookies
1/3 cup of ground nuts
135 grams of unsalted melted butter
1 can of condensed milk
1/4 cup of lemon juice
1 teaspoon of vanilla extract

Preparation:

1. Mix the crushed cookies, ground nuts, and melted butter. Place in a detachable mold and press to form the crust... set aside.

2. In a blender, place the milks and the vanilla. Blend... with the blender running, gradually add the lemon juice.

3. Pour the mixture into the crust and refrigerate for 3 to 4 hours or overnight.

Frozen Mango Pie

Ingredients:

4 ripe mangoes
2 bars of cream cheese
1 can of condensed milk (14 oz)
2 store-bought pie crusts

Preparation:

1. Remove the pulp from the mangoes and place it in the blender along with the two bars of cream cheese and the can of condensed milk.

2. Pour the mixture into the pie crusts, and you can top it with mango chunks.

3. Place them in the freezer for six hours or overnight.

Coffee Charlotte

Ingredients:

1 liter of milk
2 tablespoons of instant coffee
1 cup of sugar
1 cup of cornstarch
1 teaspoon of cinnamon
1 teaspoon of vanilla extract
3 packs of chocolate chip cookies (or your preferred chocolate chip cookies)

Preparation:

1. Mix all the ingredients in a saucepan and, over low heat, whisk continuously until it thickens from a liquid to a thick consistency. (It takes about 5 minutes to reach the desired consistency).
2. In a glass baking dish, place a layer of the mixture and then a layer of cookies, repeating the process until you finish with a top layer of cookies.
3. Refrigerate for 4 hours or overnight.

Delicious Blondie

Ingredients:

1 banana
1 teaspoon of vanilla extract
2 tablespoons of sweetener
1 tablespoon of peanut butter
1 egg
1 cup of oat flour

Preparation:

1. Mix all the ingredients and place them in a 15 x 10 or similar-sized baking pan.

2. Cook at 180°C for 20 to 25 minutes in the air fryer.

3. For the topping, mix 100 grams of cream cheese with a teaspoon of peanut butter and sweetener drops to taste.

Three-Ingredient Microwave Coconut Flan

Ingredients:

1 egg

3 tablespoons of unsweetened Greek yogurt

1 tablespoon of shredded coconut

1 tablespoon of erythritol, stevia, or sweetener of your choice

Preparation:

1. Beat the egg in a microwave-safe cup. Add the Greek yogurt and mix until you achieve a smooth texture. Incorporate the shredded coconut and mix again.

2. Microwave for 1 to 2 minutes and let it cool. You can refrigerate it for a few minutes before eating.

Air Fryer Chocolate Pound Cake

Ingredients:

1/2 cup of Greek yogurt

3 eggs

1/3 cup of sugar

1 teaspoon of vanilla extract

1/2 cup of oat flour

2 tablespoons of almond flour

2 tablespoons of cocoa powder

1 teaspoon of baking powder (Rexal)

1 bar of 85% cocoa chocolate

Preparation:

1. Mix the eggs, yogurt, sweetener, and vanilla. Incorporate the flours, cocoa, and powders.

2. Pour the mixture into an 11x15 cm or similar-sized mold and place it in the air fryer at 150°C for 15 to 20 minutes. Add the chocolate bar and cook for an additional 5 minutes.

Traditional Microwave Egg Flan

Ingredients:

1 cup of milk (200 ml)
2 eggs
1 tablespoon of vanilla extract
1 packet of artificial sweetener
1 teaspoon of honey or caramel

Preparation:

1. Add the tablespoon of honey or caramel to a cup and set it aside.

2. In another container, mix the milk with the eggs, vanilla, and artificial sweetener. Pour the mixture into the cup with the caramel.

3. Microwave for one to one and a half minutes, then let it cool for a few minutes before unmolding.

Eggless and Flourless Chocolate Brownie

Ingredients:

2 very ripe bananas
3 tablespoons of cocoa powder (125 grams)
Walnuts and chocolate chips

Preparation:

1. Mix all the ingredients until you have a paste, and place it in a mold lined with wax paper. (Using a blender yields a smoother texture).

2. Cook in an air fryer at 180°C for 20 to 25 minutes.

Banana and Coconut Bread

Ingredients:

1 egg
1 dash of vanilla extract
1 banana
1 tablespoon of brown sugar
2 tablespoons of shredded coconut
2 tablespoons of oat or almond flour
1 teaspoon of baking powder (Rexal)

Preparation:

1. Mix all the ingredients in a bowl until well integrated, then transfer the mixture to a microwave-safe mold.

2. Microwave for 1 minute and a half to 2 minutes.

3. You can decorate it with chocolate syrup as a topping.

Coconut Cookies

Ingredients:

1/2 cup of shredded coconut

2 eggs

1 tablespoon of melted coconut oil

1 tablespoon of sweetener Vanilla extract

Zest of two lemons

Preparation:

1. Mix all the ingredients well to form small patties, which you place on a baking sheet previously greased or lined with parchment paper.

2. In an air fryer at 180°C for 10 minutes or until they are firm and golden.

Express Blueberry Cheesecake

Ingredients:

1/4 cup of oats (30 grams)
1/2 banana
1/2 cup of Greek yogurt
1/2 cup of cream cheese
1/2 lemon
1 packet of stevia
30 grams of blueberries

Preparation:

1. Cover an individual small mold with a piece of plastic wrap.

2. Mix the banana well with the oats, which will serve as the base of the cheesecake. Place the mixture in the mold and set aside.

3. Mix the yogurt with the cream cheese, lemon juice, stevia, and blueberries. Add the mixture to the mold and refrigerate for two hours or overnight.

Mega Chocolate Cookie in the Air Fryer

Ingredients:

1 cup of peanut butter

1 egg

1 teaspoon of liquid sweetener or granulated sweetener

1/2 teaspoon of vanilla extract

2 to 3 tablespoons of hazelnut cream (optional)

Preparation:

1. Mix all the ingredients except the hazelnut cream. Divide the resulting dough into two equal parts.

2. Use one part of the dough to cover the bottom of a 15 cm mold and add a few tablespoons of hazelnut cream on top of the mixture before covering it with the remaining dough.

3. Cook in an air fryer at 180°C for 20 to 25 minutes.

Oat Pancakes Stuffed with Hazelnut Cream

Ingredients:

3 eggs

1 packet of stevia (artificial sweetener)

1 1/4 cups of milk (300 ml)

2/3 cup of melted butter (80 grams)

1 1/2 cups of oat flour

1 tablespoon of baking powder (Rexal) Hazelnut cream

Preparation:

1. Freeze hazelnut cream discs on a tray covered with parchment paper and set aside.

2. Separate the egg whites from the yolks of the three eggs. Mix the yolks with sweetener and add the milk, melted butter, vanilla extract, and finally, the oat flour and baking powder.

3. Beat the egg whites until stiff peaks form and gradually fold them into the previous mixture with gentle, folding motions. This will make the pancakes fluffy.

4. Pour the mixture onto a medium heat skillet, place a previously frozen hazelnut cream disc on top, cover it with more mixture, and flip the pancake to finish cooking the other side.

Reese's Pancakes

Ingredients:

1 egg
1/4 cup of Greek yogurt
1/2 banana
1/4 cup of milk
1/2 cup of oat flour
2 tablespoons of cocoa powder
1 teaspoon of baking powder (Rexal) Optional
sweetener

Preparation:

1. Mix all the ingredients well, and using a spoon, pour the mixture onto a medium heat skillet greased with cooking spray. Cover it with a lid and flip it when the edge turns golden.

2. Serve it with a tablespoon of peanut butter, banana slices, and chocolate syrup.

Baked Apple Oatmeal Bowl

Ingredients:

1/2 apple
2 eggs
1/2 cup of oat flakes
Cinnamon and Stevia to taste

Preparation:

1. Place all the ingredients in a blender until everything is well combined. Pour the mixture into an oven-safe dish.

2. Cook at 180°C for 15 minutes in the air fryer.

Lemon Cookies

Ingredients:

2 eggs
5 ml of olive oil
Lemon zest
120 grams of coconut flour
10 grams of artificial sweetener

Preparation:

1. Mix all the ingredients until you have a dough with a consistency that allows you to shape the cookies.

2. Place the cookies on a container lined with parchment paper and cook them in the air fryer for 10 minutes at 176°C.

Air Fryer Oat Churros

Ingredients:

1 cup of water
2 tablespoons of oil
A pinch of salt 1 cup of oat flour

Preparation:

1. Put water, oil, and salt in a pan over medium heat. Once the water boils, remove it from the stove and quickly stir in the cup of oat flour. Mix vigorously until the dough comes away from the pan.

2. Fill a pastry bag with the mixture and on the aluminum foil placed in the air fryer, make small holes with a knife. Place churros using the pastry bag and cook for 15 minutes at 200°C. Sprinkle with sugar.

Apple Slice Pancakes

Ingredients:

1 egg
1/3 cup of milk
1/2 cup of oat flour
1 tablespoon of baking powder
1 tablespoon of cinnamon 1 apple

Preparation:

1. Mix all the ingredients and set aside.

2. Cut the apple into slices and remove the seeds. Dip each slice into the mixture until completely covered.

3. Cook in a skillet over medium heat on both sides. Serve with fruit and honey or maple syrup.

Lemon and Blueberry Crumble Pie

Ingredients:

1/3 cup of butter
3 eggs
1/2 cup of sugar
Zest of 1 lemon
Juice of 1/2 lemon
1 1/3 cups of almond flour
1/2 cup of coconut flour
1 teaspoon of baking powder
Blueberry jam
Crumble Ingredients:
2 tablespoons of butter 1/2 cup of almond flour 1
tablespoon of sugar 2 tablespoons of coconut
flour

Preparation:

1. Mix the butter with sugar, eggs, lemon
    zest, and lemon juice. Combine the
    ingredients well and add the flours with
    baking powder. Pour the mixture into a

small round baking dish (10 x 10 inches), spread blueberry jam to cover the surface, and then add fresh blueberries.

2. Prepare the crumble by simply combining all the ingredients. The mixture will not be dry; it will have a slightly moist texture. Use damp hands to crumble it evenly over the blueberries.

3. Cook in an air fryer at 180°C (356°F) for 35 to 45 minutes.

Oat and Orange Pancakes

Ingredients:

1 cup of oat flour

Zest of 1 large orange

Juice of 1 large orange

2 eggs

A pinch of salt

1 teaspoon of baking powder

1 tablespoon of vanilla extract

1 teaspoon of olive oil

Preparation:

1. Mix all the ingredients in a bowl until fully incorporated.

2. In a medium-sized skillet over medium heat, greased with butter, pour 1/3-cup portions of the mixture. This recipe makes 5 pancakes.

Sugar-Free Cookie Mug Cake

Ingredients:

30 grams of oat flour
20 grams of peanut butter
1 egg
10 grams of chocolate chips
1 tablespoon of baking powder
1 packet of stevia
1 tablespoon of vanilla extract
A pinch of salt

Preparation:

1. Mix all the ingredients in a bowl until you achieve a semi-liquid texture.

2. Pour the mixture into a microwave-safe mug and place more chocolate chips on top of the mixture.

3. Microwave for 1 minute.

Air Fryer Walnut Pound Cake

Ingredients:

1/2 ripe banana

1 egg

2 tablespoons of Greek yogurt

1 teaspoon of vanilla

2 tablespoons of milk

1/2 cup of oat flour

1 teaspoon of baking powder

1 packet of stevia (artificial sweetener)

Chopped walnuts

Preparation:

1. Mix all the ingredients and pour them into an oven-safe mold with chopped walnuts on top.

2. Cook in an air fryer at 160°C (320°F) for 15 minutes.

Banana Pancake in Skillet

Ingredients:

1 banana, sliced
1 egg
50 ml of milk
1 teaspoon of vanilla extract
1/3 cup of rice flour

Preparation:

1.   Grease a skillet and place the banana slices in it.

2.   Mix the egg, milk, vanilla extract, and rice flour well, then pour it over the banana slices in the skillet.

3.   Cook with a lid over low heat for 4 minutes. Flip it and cook for an additional 2 minutes.

4.   Serve with granola and peanut butter.

Peanut Bread

Ingredients:

2 eggs
2 tablespoons of peanut butter
2 tablespoons of pumpkin seeds or your choice of
seeds
1 tablespoon of baking powder

Preparation:

1. Mix all the ingredients without
    overmixing.

2. Pour the mixture into a greased oven-safe
    dish.

3. Cook in the microwave on maximum
    power for 2 minutes.

Ideal to accompany savory dishes. The mixture
may be enough for two small loaves or one
medium-sized loaf.

1-Minute Apple Flan

Ingredients:

1 medium yellow apple
1 tablespoon of Greek yogurt
1 egg

Preparation:

1. Cut the apple into small pieces and
    microwave for 2 minutes. Mash it and mix
    it with the yogurt and egg.

2. Pour the mixture into a microwave-safe
    dish and cook for 1 minute.

3. You can use cinnamon or hazelnut cream
    as toppings.

French Almond Cake

Ingredients:

6 eggs at room temperature (IMPORTANT)
1 tsp salt
250 g powdered sugar / icing sugar
150 g unsalted butter, very soft, at room temperature
300 g almond flour
40 g sliced almonds for decoration

Preparation:

1. Beat the eggs, salt, and powdered sugar with an electric mixer until it becomes clear, fluffy, and you can draw a pattern with a stream on the mixture that stays for a while before incorporating again.

2. Add the butter one tablespoon at a time with the machine at minimum speed and continue to beat until incorporated.

3. Remove the mixer and gradually add the almond flour, mixing with a spatula in folding motions. Be careful not to deflate the mixture too much.

4. Transfer the mixture to a greased and parchment paper-lined springform pan, greased on top as well. Level it with a spoon.

5. Decorate with sliced or finely chopped almonds. Do not toast them because they will toast in the oven.

6. Bake in an air fryer at 170°C/340°F for 30-40 minutes or until it is golden on top, and you can insert a toothpick and it comes out clean.

7. Once cooled, decorate with more powdered sugar.

Single Serving Berry Bread

Ingredients:

30 grams of oat flour

1 packet of stevia

1/2 teaspoon of baking powder

1 egg

1 egg white

1 teaspoon of vanilla extract

1/4 cup of Greek yogurt Mixed berries

Preparation:

1. First, mix the dry ingredients, and then add the remaining ingredients, with the mixed berries going in last.

2. Place the mixture in an ovenproof dish previously greased with olive oil.

Cream Cheese Pound Cake

Ingredients:

4 eggs
350 grams of cream cheese
800 grams of sugar
180 grams of heavy cream

Preparation:

1. Mix all the ingredients in a bowl using a mixer.

2. Pour the mixture into an ovenproof mold lined with parchment paper.

3. Bake in an air fryer at 180°C for 45 minutes.

KITCHEN CONVERSIONS CHART TABLE

Volumes

A PINCH	1/16 TSP
A DASH	1/8 TSP
1 TSP	5 ML
1 TBP	15 ML
1 CUP	240 ML

Volumes By Weight

ONE POUND = 454 GRAMS = 3 1/2 CUPS FLOUR = 2 1/2 CUPS SUGAR

Temperatures

212°F	100°C
225°F	110°C
250°F	130°C
275°F	140°C
300°F	150°C
325°F	170°C
350°F	180°C
375°F	190°C
400°F	200°C
425°F	220°C
450°F	230°C
475°F	240°C

Cup	Tbsp	Tsp
1/4	4	12
1/3	5	16
1/2	8	24
2/3	11	32
3/4	12	36
1	16	48

BAKING WITHOUT FLOUR